PAINT
PLAY

W0008928

LOM
ART

Artwork and instructions by Katie Rose Johnston
Edited by Jocelyn Norbury
Designed by Claire Clewley
Cover design by John Bigwood

First published in Great Britain in 2019 by LOM ART, an imprint of
Michael O'Mara Books Limited, 9 Lion Yard, Tremadoc Road, London SW4 7NQ

W www.mombooks.com/lom
f Michael O'Mara Books
y @OMaraBooks
O @lomartbooks

Copyright © Michael O'Mara Books Limited 2019

All rights reserved. No part of this book may be reproduced, stored in a
retrieval system, or transmitted in any form or by any means, without the prior
permission in writing of the publisher, nor be otherwise circulated in any form
of binding or cover other than that in which it is published and without a similar
condition including this condition being imposed on the subsequent purchaser.

A CIP catalogue record for this book is available from the British Library.

ISBN: 978-1-910552-87-2

10 9 8 7 6 5 4 3 2 1

Printed in May 2019 by Leo Paper Products Ltd, Heshan Astros Printing Limited, Xuantan
Temple Industrial Zone, Gulao Town, Heshan City, Guangdong Province, China.

KATIE ROSE JOHNSTON

PAINT PLAY

21 EASY WATERCOLOUR TECHNIQUES TO EXPLORE

ABOUT THE ARTIST

Katie Rose Johnston is a multi-disciplinary illustrator based in London. She has been painting with watercolour for as long as she can remember, using bold shapes, quick marks and colourful layers to push the boundaries of its pretty reputation.

Katie has an MA in Visual Communication from the Royal College of Art and alongside her commercial projects teaches workshops that explore paint, pattern and place. *Paint Play* is her first book.

CONTENTS

"HAVE NO FEAR OF PERFECTION — YOU'LL NEVER REACH IT."

SALVADOR DALÍ

SPLASH, SPLATTER, SWOOSH

If you mention watercolour to most people, the chances are that the first thing they think of will be traditional landscape paintings. This is far from the only use for water-based paints, though. There is a whole world of playful, colourful and modern techniques that don't require art-school training.

The simple, effective ideas in this book require very few materials and are easy enough to be created by anyone, whatever their ability or experience.

Whether you want to discover a new approach that will add an extra element to your painting or just get messy and have fun, you'll find something here to spark your imagination. Use the artwork in this book as inspiration or practise the techniques independently – it's up to you.

Throw away the rule book, grab some paints and experiment with texture, colour and shape. Try some of these methods with gouache or acrylic paint, too – just add lots of water!

GETTING STARTED

Here's a basic guide to the materials you need to start your watercolour journey.

PAINT

All of the techniques in this book are designed to be practised with watercolour paint, either solid or from a tube. Some also work well with acrylics or gouache if diluted with lots of water. Each technique is 'colour coded' in the bottom right-hand corner to show the types of paint that can be used – a green circle means you can use gouache, a red circle means you can experiment with acrylics.

Acrylic

Gouache

BRUSHES

Start with a set that has some fine, pointed brushes in a few different sizes and a selection of flat and angled brushes. Don't spend a lot of money at this stage. You will discover your favourites as you experiment with different techniques and painting styles.

MIXING PALETTE

A plastic palette with separate mixing wells is useful, as it allows you to mix up lots of colours at once.

PAPER

There are lots of types of paper you can use with water-based paint. To start with, it might be best to choose one that is made for watercolour, so it can absorb a lot of liquid without getting soggy or disintegrating.

It's best to use paper that is at least 250gsm (grams per square metre) and has a textured surface — not too absorbent but not too smooth.

SPONGES

Different types of sponges are useful for creating texture and for 'blotting' paint.

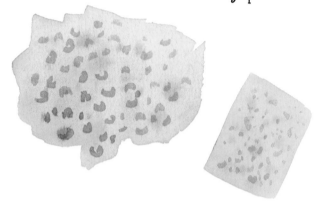

HARD PENCILS AND A SOFT ERASER

Use pencils with a hard lead if you want to lightly sketch out your shapes before painting. Watercolour is transparent, so don't press too hard or the pencil lines will show. You can use an eraser to gently rub out the lines once the paint has dried.

WAX CRAYONS

You can use these to repel watercolour pigment.

MASKING FLUID

This can be painted on to paper to 'mask off' specific areas, leaving them paint-free.

LAYERING COLOURS

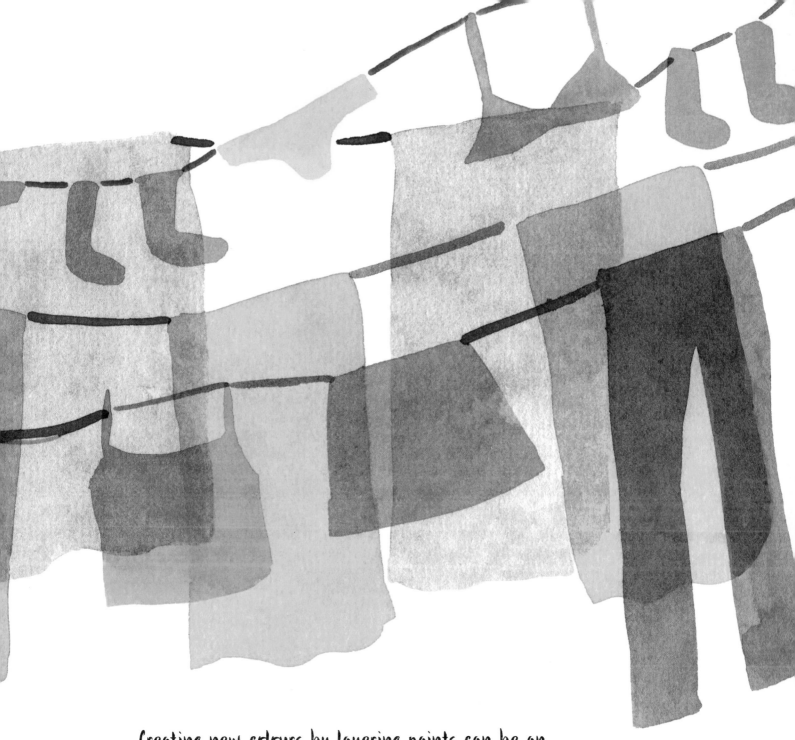

Creating new colours by layering paints can be an
interesting alternative to mixing pigments in your palette.

COLOUR COMBINATIONS

As long as you use good-quality paper, you can mix colours by layering two pigments on top of one another.

Green and blue = teal

Even unexpected colour combinations can work well.

Wait until the first layer is completely dry before painting another colour over the top.

Blue and yellow make green.

Recall how primary colours are mixed to predict the colours you will end up with when you layer one over another.

Red and yellow make orange.

Use red and blue for purple.

Varying the amount of pigment in one or both of the colours in the mix creates different shades.

TONAL LAYERING

Using one pigment mixed with different amounts of water will create completely different shades for layering.

The range of shades that can be produced from one pigment is incredible.

learning to layer colours will be useful for any work you do with water-based paint.

Paint the lightest objects first, using pigment diluted with plenty of water.

– – – – – –

Leave the first layer to dry, then add more pigment and paint the second layer of detail.

– – – – – –

After leaving the paint to dry for a second time, add more pigment and apply the final, darkest layer.

MIRROR IMAGES

Think up some beautiful colour combinations and see how they bleed together when you fold the paper to create magical 'mirror art'.

BUTTERFLY PRINTS

For this technique, use a lightweight paper that creases easily.

Pre-fold the paper so you can tell where the halfway point lies.

Choose two or three colours and, using a very wet brush, create a wing shape on one half, adding detail while the paint is wet.

Simple splodges

Spots and stripes

Tonal detail

Before the paint dries, fold the paper and press the two halves together.

Why not create a magical butterfly-house effect by making lots of butterflies, cutting them out and then mounting on to a background?

Leave for a minute to let the paint absorb, then unfold to reveal the butterfly. When dry, paint in the body.

DRY BRUSH TEXTURES

Use just a small amount of water and a dry brush to create a range of different textures and add detail over washes. Fur real!

BEST IN SHOW

The great thing about this technique is that there's no need to draw an outline – just dip, dab and brush.

Try dabbing the paint quickly, or loading the brush with two colours at the same time. Use tissue to remove excess paint and achieve softer effects.

Create shapes using different types of brushstrokes to add movement and character.

Mix some colours using a tiny amount of water. Use a dry brush to add the smallest amount of paint to the paper.

Short, angular marks

Smooth, elegant strokes

Thin brush, small spirals

DIFFERENT STROKES

Round brush, rapid dabs

Large, round, soft brush, stippling motion

Flat brush, horizontal and vertical strokes

Flat brush strokes in one direction

Coarse, round brush, stippling motion

Two colours, flat brush, wavy strokes

Wide flat brush and sweeping strokes

Use a fine, pointed brush to add detail once dry.

Round brush dabs

Dry brush work creates texture, and is great when painting natural materials such as wood and stone.

WET-ON-WET REFLECTIONS

Dip a toe into this wet-on-wet technique to create a shimmering lake that you'll want to dive right into.

MAKING A LAKE

Start with a simple base shape in a light wash, add layers of pigment, then 'drop in' colour to create a watery reflection.

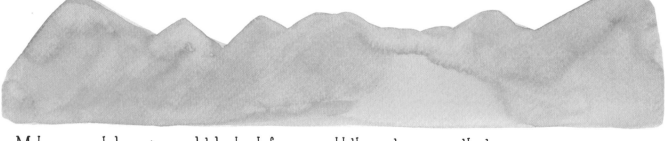

Make sure each layer is completely dry before you add the next one over the top.

Add another layer of mountains in a mid-green.

Use a darker green and a pointed brush to add trees.

Paint a crystal-clear, ice-blue wash.

Keep this layer very wet, so when the next colour is added they bleed together.

Starting with a light colour and layering darker shades on top will add depth to your picture.

Drop the lightest green pigment into the blue wash, mirroring the shape of the mountains. Add the mid-green and dark-green pigments in smaller quantities.

Tilt your paper so the colour bleeds down into the lake.

Add a fiery sun in red and drop in the reflection.

Use a dry brush and blue pigment to add ripples.

When the lake is dry, finish by adding some hills in the foreground.

GRADUATED WASHES

Use coloured water washes in two different shades to create perfectly blended backgrounds.

FADE OUT

Sketch out a skyline in pencil, then use masking tape to protect this area before adding the background wash.

Wet the whole page with a clear water wash.

Starting at the top of the page and working down towards the middle, add pink pigment using a wide brush and sweeping, horizontal strokes.

Starting from the bottom, do the same with blue pigment, until the colours meet in the middle. The wet paper will blend the colours.

When the 'ombre' background is dry, remove the masking tape and paint in the city skyline.

Layer small details, waiting for each layer of paint to dry before adding more.

Use square-edged brushes for the roofs. Keep it simple.

MIXING COLOURS

Try the same technique with three or even four colours – be inspired by dramatic sunsets and moody twilights.

GRADUATED WASHES AREN'T JUST FOR BACKGROUNDS

OMBRE BRUSHSTROKES

Get this effect by squeezing two or more colours straight from the tube onto a palette, keeping them close enough to load the brush with one dip.

Sketch a shape and fill it with two colours, using the same technique.

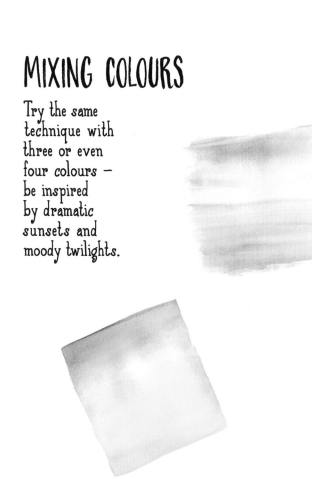

SAFARI PRINTS

Go on safari, using different patterns and layers to form leopards, tigers, zebras and more.

SKIN DEEP

Use a base-colour wash to create simple shapes. Once dry, layer up patterns over the top to create some really wild animal prints.

Use stripes and patterns to suggest the curves and muscles of the animal's body.

Thin brushes can create tiger or zebra stripes.

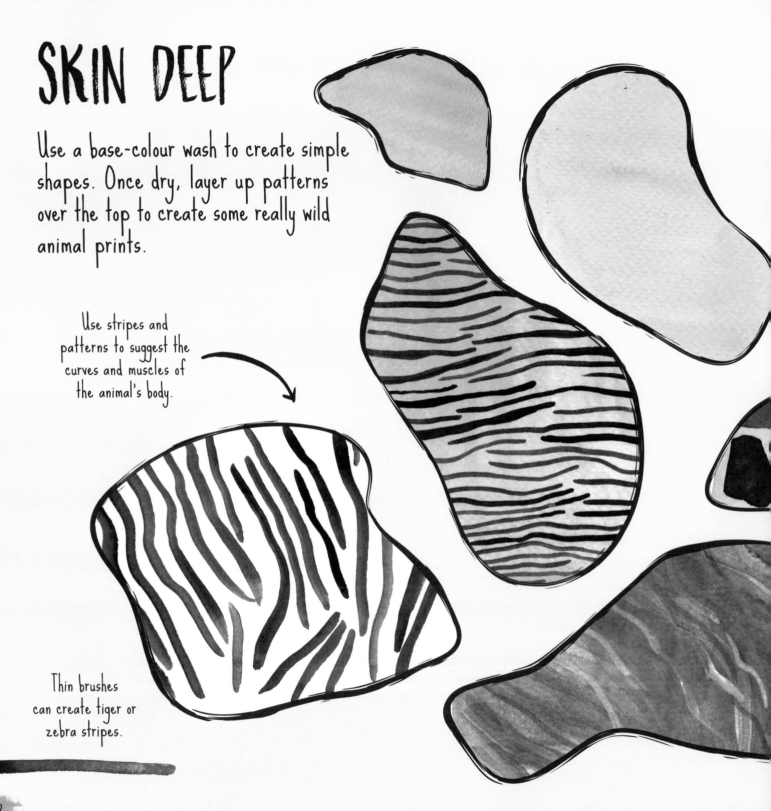

A very fine brush can be used to create the tiny scales and ridged texture of a crocodile's skin.

A square-edged brush can be dabbed to make uneven rectangles for a giraffe print.

Incomplete repeated circles create a leopard-print pattern.

Layer white paint over grey using a dry brush to create the rough skin of an elephant.

Try copying the outline shapes of the finished animals on the previous page and then fill them with these prints.

WATERCOLOUR MONO-PRINT

Mono-printing is a technique that uses inks to print an image.
Adapting the technique for paint results in some beautiful effects.

WILDFLOWER MEADOW

Using just two types of paper and some randomly placed paint splodges, the beauty of this wildflower meadow belies the simplicity of the painting process.

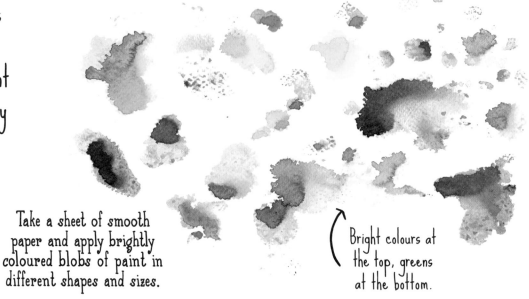

Take a sheet of smooth paper and apply brightly coloured blobs of paint in different shapes and sizes.

Bright colours at the top, greens at the bottom.

While wet, carefully place a sheet of watercolour paper over the top. Use a rolling pin so the paint spreads evenly.

Allow a few minutes for the watercolour paper to absorb the paint, then peel the sheets apart and leave to dry.

Finish with simple, handpainted stems and leaves to turn the abstract pattern into a wildflower meadow.

BRUSHSTROKE FIGURES

Painting people might sound daunting, but each of these simple silhouettes is the work of just a couple of brushstrokes.

FIGURE IT OUT

Don't worry about how a person 'should' look – just allow the brush to guide you in a single, sweeping stroke.

Use a flat, angled brush and start at the head, working down in one confident stroke.

Copy the shape of this guideline, noticing how the twists and turns of the brush create the shape.

Once you have practised a few times, try using different colours and varying shapes to create a cast of colourful characters.

Shadow and tone develop naturally when using a single colour – you can easily see how the pigment is distributed.

DIFFERENT TYPES OF BRUSHES
CREATE DIFFERENT STYLES OF OUTLINE

These figures, painted with a finer brush, have outlines that are less smooth to give the appearance of more detailed features.

TRY SOME
ALTERNATIVE SHAPES

Use the same confident strokes and a wide brush to paint a simple, stylish fruit bowl.

GESTURAL MARK-MAKING

Calligraphy isn't just about letters – use a technique called 'gestural mark-making' to paint bold, expressive scenes.

BLOSSOMING SHAPES

Let the brush dance naturally, practising quick, bold strokes to become confident in your mark-making abilities. See how graceful your lines become the more you relinquish control.

Make the blossom by using a very watery pink and a round brush. Dab in quick movements.

Keep it loose – don't worry about making a realistic tree shape at first.

Drop in a darker pink pigment to the blossom to create the multi-tonal flowers.

For the branches, mix up a very dark black – maybe even add some Indian ink to the palette.

Take time to practise creating the elegant lines of the tree branches.

Use smooth, sweeping strokes.

Branches can take on many different forms, but try to use confident strokes every time.

These gnarled-looking branches were created by wiggling the brush as it was applied to the paper.

Use similar, loose strokes, in a more structured way, to add a focal point – a Japanese pagoda.

WET-ON-WET BRUSHSTROKES

Create a glorious array of tropical feathers using different colour combinations applied to a watery base shape.

COLOURFUL FEATHERS

Create a base shape in a single colour, then paint a contrasting colour on top while the paint is wet.

Always start with a simple, single-colour base shape, then copy these colourful designs.

A very light wash with alternating spots down each side.

A strong blue outline with dark green spots down the sides.

Yellow and green 'ombre' effect with small spots of turquoise dropped in.

Different colour combinations, patterns and amounts of pigment vary the effect.

Light-green base with yellow and green stripes.

Drop in spots of green, then yellow, then blue to create the distinctive 'eye' on a peacock feather.

Adding extra pigment around the edges of the feather creates the illusion of light and shine.

When dry, use a fine, pointed brush to add a central line detail for definition.

Mix it up by starting with a base of feathery brushstrokes instead of a solid shape.

PEN ON PAINT

Add detail to watery base shapes with a pen for a modern look that's simple to achieve.

PEN DETAIL

A fun, quirky effect that is perfect if you aren't confident painting-in intricate detail.

Fill out base shapes quickly for an even finish.

Leave the base to dry before adding simple line details in fine pen.

Add simple faces.

A thick marker and short lines create a soft coat.

EXPERIMENT WITH DIFFERENT TYPES OF INK

Thin brush and ink for more tonal detail

Fineliner for a sketchy look

Felt-tip pen for a bold and quirky feel

PLAY WITH COLOUR FILL

Create an outline then fill with a repeating pattern.

Use pen to add outlines, transforming any splodgy shapes.

There's no need to stick to a realistic palette.

MASKING TAPE TILES

'Azulejos' is the Portuguese name for the ceramic tiles that can be seen around Lisbon's scenic streets. But why pack a bag when you can create your own?

THE ART OF AZULEJOS

Feel the summer vibes by using masking tape to create classic geometric designs.

Start by using masking tape to create a grid of horizontal and vertical lines on your paper.

Mix up lots of watery blue pigment then use a flat brush to sweep the first layer of paint over the page. Allow to dry thoroughly.

Next, create a diagonal grid in masking tape over the top. Repeat the process, covering the page with a blue wash.

Leave to dry, then carefully peel off your tape.

You should already have an interesting pattern, but for more detail you could create a third layer of tape and paint.

This technique works by creating more intensity of colour in each layer – so some areas that aren't covered with tape receive three layers, while other parts only get painted over once or twice.

Add floral and geometric detail using a fine, pointed brush.

SPECKLES, SPOTS AND SPATTERING

Transport yourself to a Moroccan souk using this messy trio of paint application techniques.

SIMPLE TEXTURES

Things are about to get messy. These techniques are most effective on a large scale.

Sketch out the structure of your stall using variations on a triangle shape to make spice 'mountains'.

Work in layers — paint a base colour and allow it to dry before layering your detail over the top.

Or, try leaving the base layer wet and dropping in colour so it bleeds into a soft, dotty texture like this.

SPECKLES

Choose brushes based on their shape and the coarseness of the bristles.

When you have painted your spices, add baskets to put them in. Copy this simple shape and fill with lines or cross-hatching for a woven effect.

SPOTS

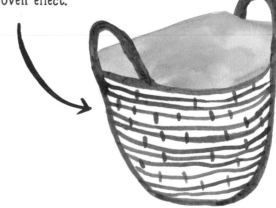

60

When spattering, you could try using a paper template to protect the rest of your painting.

A round, fine brush 'stamped' in quick movements creates this texture.

Small, square-edged brushes make angular spots.

Use angled brushes and quick dabs for this mottled effect.

Flicking the paint from the brush is fun and messy.

SPATTERING

WAX RESIST

Join the space race and revisit this simple childhood technique, using wax crayons and watercolour paints.

OUT OF THIS WORLD

Start with some simple drawings in wax crayon, then layer watercolour over the top to create a far-out space scene.

Spiral galaxy

Saturn

Mars

Using a selection of brightly coloured oil pastels or wax crayons, fill the page with as many space-themed objects as you can think of.

Next, cover the page with a clear water wash. Brush and drop red, blue, green and black paint over the top of the crayon.

Start with lighter colours and build up the pigment, adding black last.

When the paint has dried, use a coarse brush and white pigment to spatter 'stars' across your painting.

Have some tissue to hand to blot the paint away from your planets, to keep the colours vibrant.

UFO

65

CROSSHATCHING

This simple brushwork trickery can produce a wonderful range of effects.

SHADES OF GREEN

Lend depth and texture to a patchwork
of fields using some simple brush effects.

Mix up different shades
of green, adding more yellow
to some and more blue to others,
to achieve this patchwork of colour.

Use a thin,
fine brush
to build
up texture
with simple
crosshatch
in two
directions.

VERSATILE LINES

Texture can be added to all sorts of different elements — these
thatched and tiled roofs use simple crosshatching to great effect.

Experiment with lines, strokes and colours. Each will produce a different effect when layered on top of the base colour.

TREE-STYLE

Build rows of simple, straight strokes for a festive fir.

Simple strokes in different directions add movement.

Use two shades of green and a simple crosshatch pattern.

Take a break from green and try some autumnal shades.

Overlapping zig-zag lines give a looser, more natural look.

CLING FILM TEXTURES

Why stick to brushes? This super-simple method
of applying paint gives spectacular results.

CLEVER CLING FILM

Experiment with using cling film over wet paint to create a textured effect with lots of depth and movement.

Pick two paint colours.

Saturate your paper with a wash of the first colour, then drip the second over the top.

Place cling film over the page, then crease and wrinkle it.

Leave to dry, then peel off the cling film.

Folds and wrinkles create this wave effect.

Mask off details to paint in later.

As the second colour pools it will create areas of contrast.

For a slightly more pronounced two-tone effect, apply the base colour, then the cling film and wrinkle as before.

Peel back the cling film layer and pour a small amount of the second colour underneath, then replace the cling film and leave to dry.

The second colour will pool more prominently in some areas, rather than spreading across the whole page.

USING FOIL

Applying tin foil gives the same effect with harder, more defined lines.

Blue, green and turquoise make for a tropical sea.

Why not create sample sheets using different textures and colours?

FLAT BRUSH CITY

Who would have guessed you
could build a whole city using
just one brush?

SUPER SKYLINE

Use a flat brush, an even stroke and lots of layers to create a spectacular skyline with surprising depth and detail.

Start by using a wide, flat brush to lay the foundations of the buildings.

When the first layer has dried, add more brushstrokes in contrasting colours to build tone and depth.

Add windows using a narrower flat brush in single downward strokes.

ADDING PERSPECTIVE

The flat brush technique can be used creatively to experiment with perspective.

A flat brush, applied in circular strokes can create soft, 'lollipop' trees.

URBAN JUNGLE

Triangle shapes, circles, wavy lines and broken brushstrokes can be turned into different types of trees.

Add the trunk and branches in a darker colour.

WINDOW WATCHING

Even small details can be added using a flat brush.

Use the tip of the brush to make rows of small rectangles.

Introduce a different brush size.

Sketch the shape in pencil first, then fill in.

SALT COLLAGE

Use salt to create brilliant textures,
perfect for making colourful collages
and abstract patterns.

PAPER, PAINT, SALT

These are the only three ingredients you need
to create mesmerizing salt-crystal textures.

Use a wide brush to paint
a selection of paint swatches in
different colours. Bright colours
with lots of pigment work well.

Sprinkle a layer of salt over
the wash — the more you
add, the more pronounced the
effect will be.

As the paint
dries, the salt
absorbs the
water, leaving
a textured effect.

Dust off the salt
when the paint is
completely dry.

Cut abstract shapes from your
swatches and stick them on to
a coloured background. Using
collage gives you the freedom
to move your composition around.

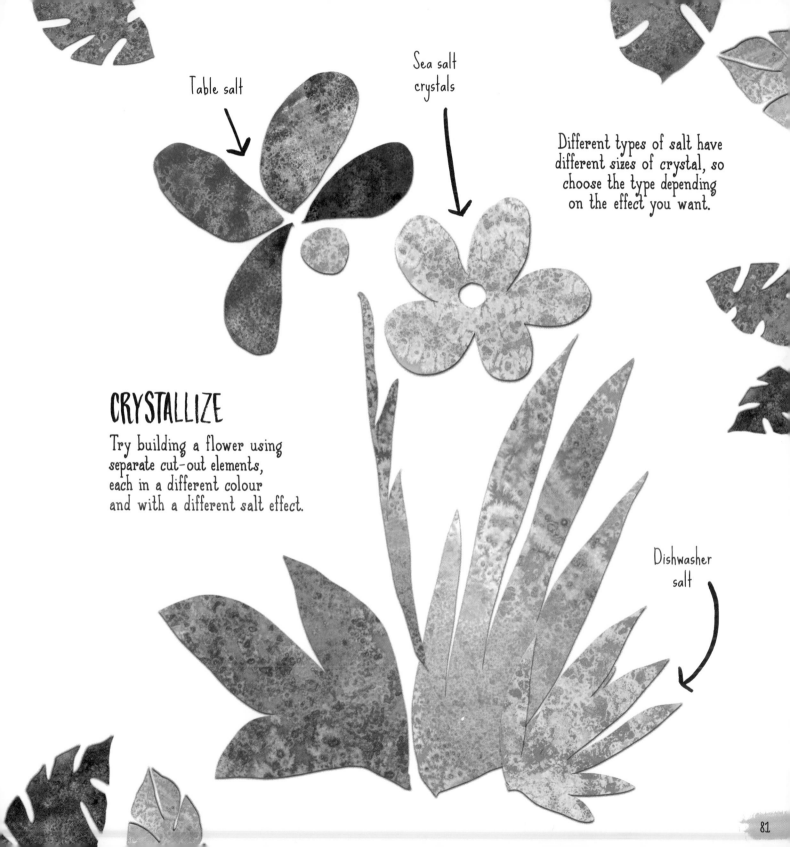

Table salt

Sea salt crystals

Different types of salt have different sizes of crystal, so choose the type depending on the effect you want.

CRYSTALLIZE

Try building a flower using separate cut-out elements, each in a different colour and with a different salt effect.

Dishwasher salt

MASKING-FLUID SWANS

Sometimes, it's not what you paint
but what you leave out that matters.

MASK IT OFF

Masking fluid, applied like paint, allows you to keep areas free from pigment so you can get creative with background effects.

Use masking fluid to paint the shapes of the swans.

Trace these outlines

When the fluid is dry, use a wide brush and sweeping, horizontal strokes to paint a blue water wash over the top.

As the paint is drying, add in some ripples using a dry brush and darker pigments such as purple and green.

Use a pointed brush to add eye and beak details to complete the face and add definition to the wings.

Use an old brush for the masking fluid and wash it immediately after use.

SIMPLE FLAMINGOS

Instead of filling the inside of a shape with masking fluid, paint the negative space around an outline and fill in with a graduated wash.

STRAW-BLOWN PAINTING

Put down your brush, grab a straw and create an explosion of colour using your brightest, boldest paints.

A RIOT OF CORAL

For best results, try not to think too much about the shapes you want to create.

Create a base to anchor your picture, then dab lots of watery blobs of colour just above it. The more liquid in your blobs, the more paint you have to blow into shapes.

Using a straw, blow upwards to create coral shapes. Experiment with different angles to guide the paint.

A narrow straw lends precision and forms intricate, 'explosive' shapes.

Use a wide straw – or improvise with a rolled up tube of paper – to make bolder, thicker lines.

AQUATIC ADVENTURES

Create jellyfish by painting a semi-circle and blowing the paint in one direction to leave trailing tendrils.

Anything with branches or spindly arms can be created using this technique.

A messy page of paint explosions can be refined with details once dry.

NO FISHING!

MIXED TECHNIQUE GREENHOUSE

Make use of a few different techniques to create a tropical sensation.

HOTHOUSE HEAVEN

All of the plants start with a shape in a single colour and 'build up' in simple stages.

THREE POINTY OVALS IN LIME

Layer a contrasting colour on one half of each leaf.
Add delicate lines with a thin brush when the base is dry.

ONE DARK-GREEN OVAL

Drop in yellow pigment while the base is wet. Then
use a dry brush to add spots of dark green and brown.

A FEW SPIKY SHAPES IN MID-GREEN

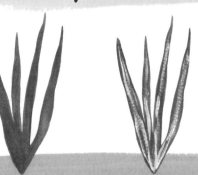  

Add dry brushstrokes of white pigment over the base colour, once dry.

FIVE FINGERS IN BRIGHT GREEN

When the base is dry, create texture by adding dry brush dots and dabs in white and yellow.

SEPARATE YELLOW-GREEN LEAVES

Embellish with spots while the base is wet, then add sweeping strokes for the stems.

ADD EXTRA DETAILS

Simple flowers

Patterned plant pots

Dark green along the edges of leaves for tone

GLOSSARY

ACRYLIC PAINT A fast-drying paint made of pigment combined with a synthetic emulsion. Waterproof when dry.

BLOT To use a tissue or sponge to absorb excess moisture from a painting.

DRY BRUSH A paint application technique using a dry brush and undiluted paint for a textured effect.

GOUACHE An opaque, water-based paint. It can be diluted to resemble watercolour and is a good option when vibrant colours are required.

OMBRE A graduated blend of two or more colours.

PIGMENT A substance that gives colour to all types of paint.

WATERCOLOUR Refers to both the paint type and work created using it. Watercolour paint is semi-transparent and comes in tubes or as solid 'cakes' of pigment.

WASH A semi-transparent layer of colour applied evenly across a page. A background wash is the foundation of many watercolour techniques.

WET-ON-WET The practice of applying fresh paint to a surface or wash that is still wet. The technique can be used with watercolour, acrylic and gouache paints to produce a blurry, muted effect.